HEL
A GIRL

MW00942242

Author Links:

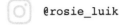

@rosie_luik

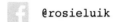

@rosieluik

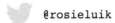

@rosieluik

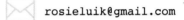

rosieluik@gmail.com

www.rosieluik.com

CONTENTS

DEDICATION

This book is dedicated to my amazing kids Ava, Aston, Coco and Elvie.

You all inspire me and challenge me in the most wonderful ways and it's because of you four that I wrote/produced/created this book.

Ava, my first born, thank you for your questions, your honesty and having "no filter" during our conversations about vaginas and all other things. Thanks for the laughs we have shared together whilst writing and for your no-nonsense attitude. You truly mean the world to me.

My husband, you're my rock and my everything. Thanks for the constant motivation and for always being my voice of reason.

And as always, thank you to all the girls that entrust me with their questions, I'm honoured by your continued support and hope that this book brings you comfort.

"A GIRL SHOULD BE TWO THINGS, CLASSY AND FABULOUS"

— Coco Chanel

PREFACE

Throughout this book, I have placed the most valuable advice and quotes from women everywhere. I asked them, having been through puberty, what advice would they give their 12-year-old self again, as well as the inspiring quotes they use in everyday life. I hope to inspire you; I hope you walk away with something valuable that you can use in your own life and eventually pass on as advice to someone else.

HELLO

My name is Rosie and it's really nice to meet you! I wrote this book for all of you girls out there who are going through puberty. I was hoping that sharing my personal stories may give you peace of mind and also give you a bit of a laugh when it comes to those embarrassing moments my friends and I have been through. Most importantly though, I wanted to give you this book to show you that you are not alone — that, no matter what you're going through, someone else has been there and made it through to the other side, just like you will too.

Think of this book as your safe haven, a guide to help you deal with all the questions, anxiety, curiosity and emotions that come with puberty.

The first thing I want you to know is that what you are experiencing is completely **NORMAL**.

The second thing I want you to know is that **YOU** ARE **NOT** ALONE. Every single person goes through puberty at some point in their lives... including me!

Puberty can seem overwhelming, embarrassing and even really scary. Don't worry though — with this book you will learn about what's happening to your body and emotions and understand why it's happening. I will share some fun facts along the way, as well as some of my favourite personal quotes that really helped me and still do.

So, let's jump in and get started.

"DON'T BE AFRAID TO FAIL, BE AFRAID NOT TO TRY"

WHAT IS PUBERTY EXACTLY?

Puberty is when a child begins to become an adult. As your body changes to become sexually mature, by this I mean giving you the ability to reproduce or get pregnant, you will start having your period. Puberty is the transformation from childhood, the state of being a child, to adolescence or pre-adulthood; in your case, from a girl to a woman.

That might sound a little scary, but your body doesn't change overnight; it happens over a period of time.

When it's time for puberty to start, the brain produces hormones that let the body know it's ready (hormones are chemicals that send messages throughout the body).

"KNOWLEDGE DISPELS FEAR". *This quote is so powerful and is so true, if things appear scary to you, gaining as much knowledge and information on the topic really helps put things into perspective and see them for what they really are.*

For girls, the ovaries produce a range of hormones that stimulate growth, change and sexual maturity in the body. Oestrogen and progesterone are the two main hormones that are responsible for the changes.

ESTROGENS: This name refers to a group of hormones called oestrone, oestradiol and oestriol. They help control a woman's monthly cycle (period) by helping the uterus lining grow thicker. Oestrogen also helps with blood clotting and bone formation.

PROGESTERONE: Like Oestrogen, this hormone is produced in the ovaries and helps prepare your body for future conception and pregnancy.

14

Puberty starts at different ages for everyone, although typically it begins between the ages of 8 and 13 years old and finishes between the ages of 15 and 17. However, it's completely normal to happen outside these ages too.

During puberty, lots of things in the body change, grow and develop.

In the next few chapters, we will talk about these changes and what you can expect.

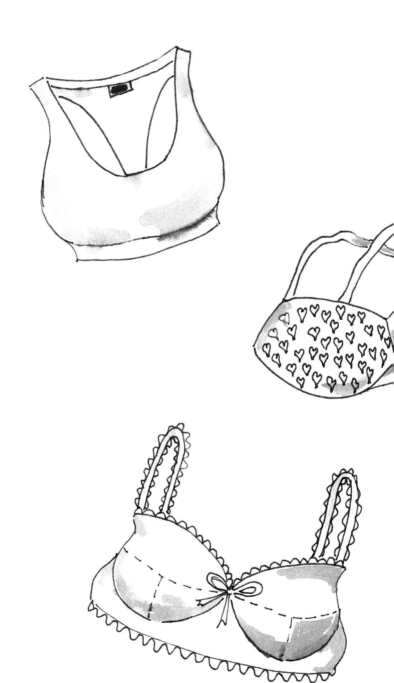

CHANGES TO YOUR BREASTS

During puberty your breasts will begin to grow and develop. This happens at different times for everyone and in different ways.

With me, I noticed small bumps were starting to form under my nipples; they were tender and sore to touch. I was a little worried at first, but then I found out that this was a sign that my breasts were growing and completely normal.

Around your nipple is your areola — this may change in colour and may grow bigger as well.

Your breast buds will start to get round and

full, eventually shaping out into your breasts.

The milk ducts will also develop in preparation should you decide to have a baby one day. After the baby is born your breasts will have the ability to then produce milk from the milk ducts.

Just remember that this process can happen slowly or quickly. You may notice that some of your friends have big breasts and some have smaller breasts. The important thing to remember is that breast changes are different for everyone and your body will change the way it's meant to, for you. To help you feel a little more confident about your growing breasts, you might also want to think about buying a training bra.

I was so embarrassed to ask my mum for a bra; I was 13 and everyone at school was already wearing them, but I didn't see the point because my breasts were always quite small. But then one day a boy walked past me at school and said "Hey, you can see through your top you know." It didn't bother me because, really, there was nothing much to see, but it did make me feel a little self-conscious and I ended up asking my mum to buy me a training bra. The conversation wasn't embarrassing and I remember feeling really special and important having my mum take me out especially to choose a bra.

18

FUN FACT: *In Ancient times before bras were invented, Roman women used to bandage their breasts in place for support. The very first modern style bra was made from handkerchiefs and invented in November 1914.*

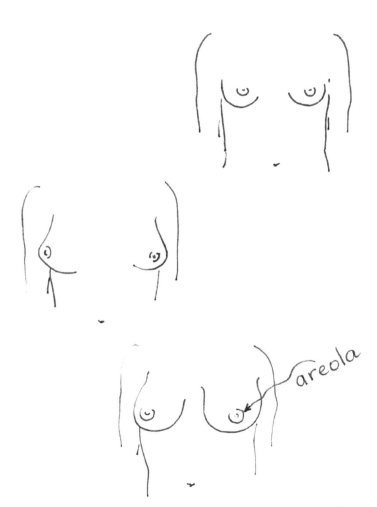

areola

YOUR GROWING BODY

During puberty, you will see a change in your height. Your weight will also change and your hips will become wider.

This all helps to prepare your body for carrying a baby, should you choose to have one later on.

There is no typical or "right" shape for your body. You and your friends will be different in the way that your bodies grow and develop.

Just remember that you are unique and you will have the exact body shape that is right for you. Emotionally you may be uncomfortable with the changes: you may get self-conscious that your hips look bigger than your friend's, or that your breasts may appear smaller. You may feel like you are too skinny or not skinny enough. These feelings are all a normal part of going through puberty. Remember that your friends are all probably feeling the exact same way!

I want you to know that you are beautiful, you are unique and you are simply amazing! You will grow and develop as you are supposed to. You'll learn to embrace who you are and who you are going to be. As much as this might be a scary time, this is also an incredible time, where you can see just how amazing your body and you can be.

HAIR

No, I'm not talking about the hair on your head.

You will start to notice that the hair all over your body will get longer, thicker and darker; AND you will start to grow hair in places you didn't think possible, like your underarms and pubic area.

Pubic hair usually starts to grow along the vaginal lips and above your pubic bone. You may notice it becoming darker and thicker over time. Pubic hair can be curly, straight, thick, fine, coarse or smooth and come in various colours too. Again, it's all normal and everyone is different.

Your leg and underarm hairs will start to grow as well and you may choose to shave them or not — it's completely up to you and what you feel comfortable with.

I decided I wanted to shave my legs at the age of 12. I asked my mum and she said no, but all my friends were doing it and I eventually convinced her. I remember sitting in my bathroom alone and lathering my legs up with my dad's shaving cream. I then shaved both legs and felt so proud of myself. I did, however, need quite a few plasters as I cut myself quite a lot, so just be careful and maybe get your mum to help you the first time. It was kind of embarrassing having everyone ask how I'd hurt my legs after seeing the plasters everywhere.

FUN FACT: *The Longest pubic hair in history was 28 Inches long which is 71.7cm*

EMOTIONAL CHANGES

During puberty, your hormone levels are continuously shifting and this can result in overwhelming feelings and intense emotions. Feeling happy one moment and angry the next is completely normal; this is usually called a "mood swing".

Your body is undergoing many significant changes and you can feel overly sensitive as you try to adjust.

You may go through lots of emotions like irritability, sadness, happiness and anger. You may lose your temper easily too. You may feel self-conscious about what's happening to your body and, as crazy as it sounds, you may actually start thinking boys and or girls are CUTE! I Know! WHAT???

These emotional changes can be hard to grasp and it really helps to talk to someone you trust about how you are feeling. Maybe your Mum, Grandma, older sister, and don't forget your Dad. Sometimes you might not feel like talking to anybody and that's okay too. You may even feel more comfortable talking to your doctor or someone else who isn't related to you. If you're feeling embarrassed about opening up about your feelings, just remember that everyone goes through this and you might actually be surprised at how easy it is to just start talking.

When I was about 11 years old I was feeling really angry and upset at my Mum; she asked me to turn off the TV and I didn't want to. I was sulking in my bedroom and my brother brought me in a bowl of ice-cream to cheer me up. At first I wanted to yell at him for even coming into my room, but then when I saw what he'd brought me I couldn't help but cry. I felt very emotional and strange about feeling upset and angry and then overwhelmed and happy. I decided to talk to my Mum about how I was feeling. When she told me it was normal and all part of the hormone changes, I felt so much better.

"BE DARING,
DIFFERENT,
IMPRACTICAL,
ANYTHING
THAT WILL
INSERT
INTEGRITY &
IMAGINATIVE

VISION AGAINST
THE 'PLAY –
IT-SAFERS',
THE SLAVES
OF THE
ORDINARY."

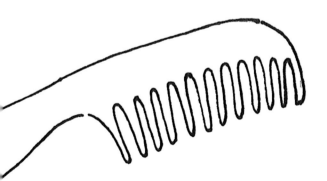

Tampon

Panty liner

Sanitary Pad

YOUR PERIOD

One of the scariest things about going through puberty is getting your period, or menstrual cycle. Again, there is no set time for this to happen. Your body will know when the time is right for you, typically between 12-14 years.

Your period usually starts with a clear discharge that you may notice in your underpants. This sometimes happens a few months before your actual period begins, so you may like to start wearing panty liners to help with keeping your undies clean.

A panty liner is a small, very thin pad that sits in your underwear.

Your menstrual cycle can be a bit tricky to understand, so I'll try and explain it simply.

The menstruation is on average a 28-day cycle and before you freak out like I did, NO YOU DON'T BLEED FOR 28 DAYS!!! Day One starts from the first day of your period.

Over those 28 days, your body will ovulate and you will have your period where you will bleed for about five to seven days.

During ovulation, the ovaries produce an egg. The egg moves down the fallopian tubes on its way to the uterus. If the egg is not fertilised by a man's sperm, pregnancy doesn't happen and the lining of the uterus comes away and exits through your vagina. This is called your period and is the reason you bleed.

The timeframe is different for everyone, so don't worry if your period only lasts two days or even if it lasts eight; this cycle is how your body prepares itself to conceive a baby.

Also, to begin with, your periods may be irregular and or light — it just depends on your body and how long it takes to get used to the changes.

You can decide to use a tampon or a pad during your period. You can even use both if you want;

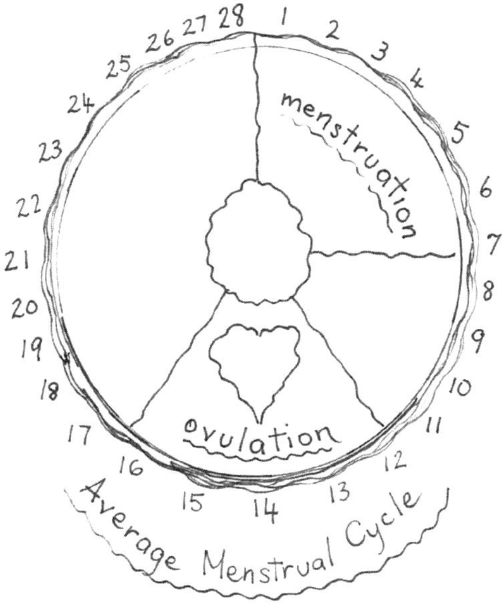

it's completely up to you! Again, don't feel pressured by your friends. Its a great idea to create a "period Kit' with the essentials – spare undies, pads and tampons inside (You can keep this safe in your school bag). Pads and tampons come in different varieties and will be suited to the type of flow you're experiencing. Heavy, medium or light.

I was the last of my friends to get my period, at 14 years old. I did feel left out as they would all talk about it and I had no idea how to be involved in the conversation. I remember feeling

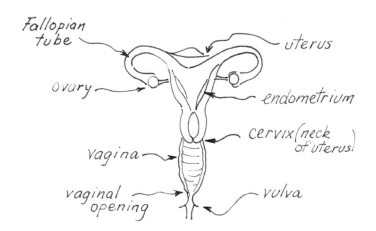

relieved when my period finally came, but in the end, it didn't really matter when I got it; I kept being told it would eventually come and it did. My periods started out light for the first few times and then became heavier as I got older.

My best friend and I made up a system where we had a code word just between us for our period. We would keep checks on each other to make sure we didn't leak on our school uniforms and we always had each other's backs. This made the whole thing so much easier and less daunting, knowing someone else was in the exact same boat as I was.

You know what too? I never used a tampon until after I had my first baby. I felt so much more comfortable using a pad; even when all my friends were using tampons, I just didn't want to. The main thing is that I did what I was comfortable with.

Experiencing pain or cramps during your period is also normal. Cramping comes from the increased production of hormones during your period. This causes the muscles in your uterus to contract and this can sometimes be painful.

You may also experience:

- Back pain
- Fatigue (feeling tired)
- Diarrhoea
- Bloating (excess fluid retention and gas, which can cause your stomach to bloat)

I've found that using a heat pack really helps ease the pain and sometimes taking pain relief medication can help too. It's important to ask an adult about this though, to be safe.

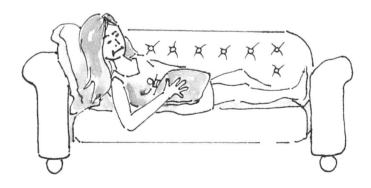

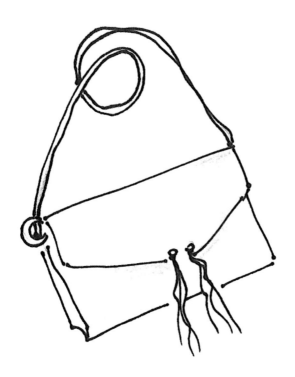

"BEAUTY IS CREATED BY YOUR ATTI-TUDE, YOUR BEHAVIOUR AND YOUR ACTIONS. IT'S ALL UP TO YOU."

PIMPLES

During puberty, you may experience those horrid little things called pimples, or even get acne.

As annoying as they are, it's normal to get pimples. They're caused by overactive glands in the skin. During puberty, these glands can produce more oil than normal and clog the skin, resulting in pimples. As well as your face, pimples can appear on your shoulders, arms, back, chest and even your butt!

The most common types of pimples are blackheads and whiteheads.

Blackheads — These pimples are black in appearance and are caused when the pores get blocked but remain open.

Whiteheads — These pimples occur when the pores open up and allow bacteria and oil to get under the skin.

I found that developing a daily skin routine and making sure I washed my face daily helped me a lot.

If your pimples get quite bad, you can talk to your doctor about using some medications to help get them under control.

You may think pimples are so embarrassing and some people are lucky enough not to get them, but they're a normal part of puberty!

FUN FACT: *Whiteheads and Blackheads are types of pimples. Boys tend to have more acne than girls because their bodies produce more oil. Pimples are caused by hormones.*

"PIMPLES,
IF YOU ARE
GOING TO
LIVE ON MY
FACE, I NEED
TO SEE SOME
RENT"

"THERE IS NO ONE LIKE YOU. YOU ARE AN ORIGINAL SO LOVE YOURSELF, YOUR UNIQUENESS AND TREASURE IT.

IT'S WHAT
MAKES YOU
SPECIAL AND
THE WORLD
NEEDS YOU
AS YOU ARE."

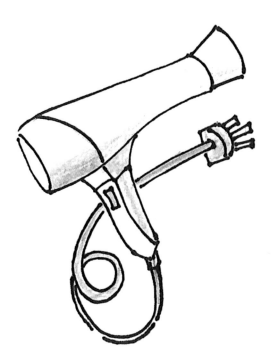

HEALTH
& EXERCISE

> **FUN FACT:** *Music has proven to improve your motivation to exercise, so crank up those tunes!! Exercise improves brain performance and memory. Exercise helps rejuvenate your body and boost your self-confidence.*

During puberty, you may find you experience a change — probably an increase — in your appetite, and that's normal. Your body is changing and growing and it's important that you make good nutritional choices during this time.

Of course, I love to eat chocolate and when I used to have sleepovers with my friends we would love to eat junk food.

Eating enough good-quality food helps with keeping your energy levels up and meeting your body's nutritional needs. I try eating three healthy meals a day along with a few snacks.

It's important that your body is getting enough vitamins and minerals when you start your period.

Getting enough iron, protein, water, calcium, folate and zinc is vital to make sure your body is growing and developing properly.

Foods like eggs, spinach, beans and meats will help maintain iron levels. Not getting enough iron can cause anaemia, which is a deficiency in red blood cells.

Protein is important in your diet because it helps your bones, organs and tissues grow. Some protein-rich foods are salmon, tuna, chicken and eggs.

Try for around three to four servings of calcium a day too. It can be found in cheese, milk and dairy products.

Zinc helps with growth and can be found in cereals, lean meats and poultry.

Folate can be found in many different fruits, grains, peas, beans, nuts, eggs cereals and vegetables. Folic acid makes red blood cells and promotes tissue growth. It's needed for the body to make RNA and DNA, which are the basic building blocks of cells. Eating food rich in folate helps maintain a healthy body.

Exercise during puberty is beneficial too. Exercising produces endorphins (happy hormones) making you feel great afterwards. Exercising can help when you are feeling sad or having a bad day; it can help relieve stress and anger as well. Exercise shouldn't be about weight loss or gain; it should be about having fun and making your body stronger and healthier. It should be enjoyable! When I was going through puberty I loved to play club netball, it was my favorite sport and form of exercise. Now I like to do Pilates and jog and I love taking a boxing class too. Don't force yourself to do something you don't enjoy; find a sport or program you like and stick to it. It's so much easier and more motivating if you do something you enjoy.

"EXERCISE BECAUSE YOU LOVE YOUR BODY, NOT BECAUSE YOU HATE IT."

HYGIENE

As you know, your hormones are in overdrive during puberty. As hair starts growing under your arms and on your vagina, those areas can get a bit smelly.

You may also notice that when you take your shoes off they can stink out your bedroom!

Your body starts producing more sweat from your sweat glands and it's important to keep yourself clean and washed.

Showering daily, making sure you wash your skin and hair regularly and washing your clothes daily helps, especially your socks and underwear.

If you are concerned about your smell, don't worry; there are heaps of products, such as deodorants and body sprays, that can help mask any odours.

FRIENDSHIPS AND PEER PRESSURE

As we get older and make our way through puberty, we start to notice how different we are from each other, how we all grow, develop and experience things at different times.

Although some of your friends may have the same opinions as you, others may not. It's important to respect everyone's individuality and understand that not everyone is thinking or doing the same as you.

Peer pressure can be a type of manipulation; it is the influence you may feel from a single person or group to do something you might not otherwise want to. It can even come from those people you think of as very close and understanding friends.

You do not have to follow the pack to fit in. Use your instincts when it comes to making certain decisions and trust how you feel. It's okay to think differently from your friends and you should never be pressured into behaving a certain way or doing something you don't want to.

Even thinking you have to buy and wear the latest clothes or have the latest smartphone or iPad can be an issue too. Being different can make you feel left out or not popular with your friends and the urge to be like them or think like them can become quite consuming.

Doing things you don't want to, just to fit in with your friends, is not okay. Yes, it's nice to feel accepted and liked but changing who you are isn't worth it. Sometimes it helps to make new friends, people who understand how you think and feel and accept you for you.

Remember: you are important and you matter. No one has the right to tell you otherwise or be disrespectful to you and your views and feelings.

Always talk to someone close to you if you are experiencing peer pressure or bullying. It's not okay and you'll find lots and lots of support and help is available. Even though it may seem like you are alone, you're not. Asking someone for advice or talking to a teacher or family member really helps.

I was bullied in both primary school and high school. I was quiet and not really into what was considered cool at the time. I tried my hardest to fit in and to like the things all my peers did — the music they listened to and the clothes they were wearing. In the end, it took me a little while but I finally made the decision to like what I like and be who I am because you get one life and trying to be someone else is just not worth it. For example, I love the band One Direction, I always have and always will. Although some people laugh at me about it (because I'm not a teenager anymore), I'm happy and that is more important than trying to impress anyone. No one else ever has the right to tell you that what you like is wrong. Just remember that there are plenty of people out there who like the same things you do. Real friends respect each other, their likes, dislikes and differences.

Being a good friend is just as important as having one. There is a quote I love and that I live my life by:

"DO NOT DIM SOMEONE ELSE'S LIGHT TO MAKE YOURS BRIGHTER"

In those times when you are feeling jealous or having ugly thoughts about your friends or so-called friends, just try to focus on doing the right thing and being a kind and loving person. Your time will come.

Friends will come and go over the years and conflict will always arise, but if you focus on being true to yourself and what you know is right, your life will take you where you need to be. Trust your gut feeling when you are deciding who to spend your time with.

Me age 11. I loved our trips to the beach as a family, looking through the rock pools catching starfish was always a favourite thing for me to do.

Me age 10. Playing board games with my brothers and sister was always a great way to have fun together!

Me age 9. My godmother is one of the most amazing
influential people in my life, I've grown up looking
up to her.

Me age 8. My first time catching yabbies was
one of my most memorable moments as a kid!

Me age 15- I didn't like photos back then.

Me age 11. Steering a ship
(pretty sure it was docked though).

Me age 15. Riding a camel on our adventures through
the outback. My family and I spent two weeks exploring the
Australian outback, it was an amazing experience.

Me age 14. My first modelling headshot.

"DON'T CHANGE
SO PEOPLE
WILL LIKE YOU.
BE YOURSELF;
THE RIGHT
PEOPLE WILL
LOVE THE
REAL YOU."

"WE WERE BORN TO BE REAL, NOT PERFECT"

SOCIAL MEDIA

FUN FACT: *In any given month, approximately 1.28 BILLION people are active on Facebook. Twitter has approximately 320 million monthly active users. Instagram has an average of over 500 million monthly active users. YouTube has over 1 Billion visitors per month.*

The influence of social media is a big issue during this time of your life. There can be pressure to have a certain phone or electronic device and even to have certain apps. It's important though to remember that if you do have access to these that they are used safely.

When I was your age we didn't have Facebook or Instagram and when you got home from school, unless you were brave enough to call the house phone of your best friend and speak to their parents to ask permission to talk, we waited until school the next day to talk to each other. Now Facebook and Instagram bring all of that home and it might seem hard to switch off or escape.

"HAPPINESS IS BEING CONFIDENTLY WEIRD"

I asked one of my good friends, who is a teenager, how she felt about social media and high school and this is what she said.

"I'm in high school and my mum and dad finally let me have a phone. I understand this is a big responsibility and I make sure I look after it. In the beginning, I thought my phone was just so I could contact my parents or family if I needed to, but when I made friends in high school I learnt all about social media and apps.

At first it seemed so overwhelming and I didn't

really see why I needed to be on Facebook or Instagram. As time went on though I felt left out; all my friends were busy posting photos, tagging each other laughing and joking together. I had absolutely no idea what was going on.

So, I talked to my mum and together we decided I could have an Instagram account, but I needed to have rules.

I am not allowed to accept friend requests from any person I haven't ever met in person.

My parents have complete access to my account.

The best piece of advice they gave me though, was that I needed to be 100% happy about photos I was posting. If my account or phone ever got hacked or one of my friends turned on me, copied a certain picture and put it up on a billboard in front of my school, I had to be sure I wouldn't be embarrassed or upset about it. I make sure none of my photos are inappropriate. It's important to think of social media as not being private, that anyone can see what you post. That really helped me when thinking about what kind of pictures I want shown. My friends and I love taking selfies and silly pictures of ourselves and I make sure it's all about having fun and a great relationship with my best friends"

FREQUENTLY ASKED QUESTIONS

When I hit puberty, I had so many questions I wanted answered, so I thought it would be a great idea to talk to girls from all over the world and ask them what questions they had about puberty too.

Kimberly asks: **"ONE BREAST IS BIGGER THAN THE OTHER. IS THIS NORMAL?".**

This is really common and it's perfectly normal. You may find your nipples or areolas look different from each other as well. During puberty, you may find your breasts grow at different rates and that's normal too. They usually even out when you get older, but it's okay if they don't. A lot of women have different-sized breasts. If you are really worried about the size difference, you can talk to your doctor about it.

Hannah asks: **"WHAT IS DISCHARGE?"**.
Vaginal discharge or secretions is fluid or mucus that leaks out of a girl's vagina. It usually begins to occur a few months before first getting your period, caused by the changes in hormones. Discharge can be thin and sticky or thick and gooey. It is usually clear in colour and helps with fighting bacteria and keeping the vagina healthy.

Josie asks: **"WHY DO YOU GET CRAMPS BEFORE AND DURING YOUR PERIOD?"**.
Cramps are caused by chemicals called prostaglandins; these chemicals cause the uterus to contract. The muscles inside the uterus contract and help push the lining out through the vagina during your period.

Xiu Chi asks: **"HOW LONG CAN YOU WEAR A TAMPON FOR?"**. *Tampons should be changed every 4-6 hours and not left in longer than 8. Overnight it is recommended to wear a pad, wearing a tampon for longer than eight hours can be dangerous.*

Sally asks: **"HOW OFTEN SHOULD I CHANGE MY PAD?".** *Changing your pad really depends on the flow of your period. If your period is light you may be able to leave your pad on for a few hours. If your period is heavy, you may find you need to change your pad more often. You should aim to change your pad every 4 hours though, as bacteria can start to grow in the blood and cause odour and infection.*

Gillian asks: **"WHY HAVEN'T I GOTTEN MY PERIOD YET? ALL MY FRIENDS HAVE?".** *The first thing you need to know is that everyone is different and we all develop at different rates. You may feel embarrassed that your friends have all gotten their periods and you haven't, but it's not a race and your period will start when your body is ready.*

Lisa asks: **"WHAT IS THE DIFFERENCE BETWEEN PIMPLES AND ACNE?".** *There is a difference between pimples and acne. Getting the occasional pimple during puberty is normal, but if these pimples become excessive and spread across your face then it's classed as acne. Acne can last a lot longer than a pimple and can become persistent. You may need to visit your doctor and get medication if you suffer from acne.*

Hannah asks: **"CAN I GO SWIMMING WHEN I HAVE MY PERIOD?".** *You can absolutely go swimming when you have your period; you just need to use a tampon. If you use a pad while you're in the water, it won't absorb any leakage and will turn soggy. If you are self-conscious about using a tampon, you can always wear board shorts or dark-coloured swimwear.*

Melanie asks: **"MY PERIOD IS IRREGULAR. IS SOMETHING WRONG?".** *When you are just starting your period, this is very common. Your body is trying to get used to all the changes happening and can cause your period to be light or irregular. Stress can also be a factor, so try not to worry about it at all, because it's completely normal. If you are really concerned, you can always talk to a doctor about what's going on.*

Teagan asks: **"WHY DON'T I HAVE PUBIC HAIR YET?".** *Some girls will grow pubic hair early and some, much later. The best thing to do is not worry about it. You will grow pubic hair when your body is ready to. You might find your underarm hair grows first, and that is completely normal.*

Whitney asks: **"WHY ARE THERE SO MANY DIFFERENT TYPES OF PADS AND TAMPONS?".** *Tampons and pads will come in a range of different sizes; this is to suit what type of "flow" you are having. The first few days of your period are usually regular so a regular tampon or a regular pad can be used. During the third to fourth day your flow is usually quite heavy and you can choose to use a tampon or pad that is more absorbent, suitable for a heavy flow. During the last few days of your period, you will find it's quite light and you may choose to use a low-flow tampon or panty liner instead of a pad. It depends on you and your body as well. If you find your entire period is light or your entire period is heavy, it's okay and you can choose to use the products that are right for you.*

Jade asks: **"WHAT DO I DO WITH MY USED TAMPON OR PAD?"**. *You will find that all public toilets are equipped with sanitary bins, so when you are out and about it's easy to dispose of your tampon and pad. The bin sits next to the toilet and is emptied regularly. Never flush a pad or tampon down the toilet. If I am at home, I always wrap my used tampon or pad up in toilet paper and place it in the bin.*

Michaela asks: **"DOES GETTING MY PERIOD MEAN I CAN CARRY A BABY?"**. *Getting your period is your body's way of telling you that you can now reproduce. The eggs from your ovaries release every month and this means that you can get pregnant and have a baby. Although there are a lot of other factors that need to be taken into consideration when preparing for a baby, it essentially means your body can physically carry a baby.*

Kylie asks: **"WHAT SHOULD I DO IF I GET MY PERIOD AT SCHOOL?".** *Firstly, don't stress out; it's all okay, and plenty of people have been through this experience. Keeping a period kit in your school bag is always a great idea. Fill a pencil case with a pad, tampon and spare underwear and keep it tucked away in your school bag. Then, if your period does come you're prepared. If you don't have any supplies on you, the school office will and it's okay to go and ask for some help or supplies. If you have leaked in your underwear or on your uniform, try not to panic. The office should have a spare uniform you could borrow or it might be one of those times you need to call your mum, aunty, sister or even your dad and ask them for help! Don't be embarrassed. I guarantee they have been through it all before too.*

Rachel asks: "I FEEL SAD A LOT. IS THIS NORMAL?". *Feeling sad is normal, mostly because all of the hormones in your body are going crazy. However, there is something called depression and that can affect your eating and sleeping abilities, how you act and your everyday life. Depression goes deeper than just feeling sad. If you think you are overly sad, having trouble sleeping and it's happening most days, you should talk to a parent or guardian about it all. There are so many things available to help you feel like yourself again.*

Rebecca asks: "I FEEL HUNGRY ALL THE TIME. IS THIS NORMAL?". *During puberty, your body does a lot of growing and, in order for it to keep up, it requires fuel; that fuel is food. Just make sure you are making good food choices and giving your body the right kind of nutrients to keep it strong and healthy.*

Peta asks: **"I FEEL LIKE I HAVE NO ONE TO TALK TO ABOUT PUBERTY, I'M SO EMBARRASSED?".** *Puberty can be an embarrassment and that's why I wanted to create this book — so you know you aren't alone and what you are going through is normal. Sometimes you might have to be brave and take the first step in talking to someone. You will be surprised how easy it is to ask questions and once you start you won't want to stop. Ask as many questions and start as many conversations with your family or doctor as you can. Remember, EVERYONE goes through puberty.*

Darcey asks: **"WHEN SHOULD I BUY A BRA?".** *Buying a bra can be a daunting task and it's completely up to you and what you feel comfortable with. A sports bra is a great place to start — it can give you support and provide comfort while your breasts are growing and developing. If you are self-conscious about your growing breasts, a sports bra can really help with gaining your confidence back.*

Lucy asks: **"WHY DOES MY BODY HAVE TO CHANGE SO MUCH?".** *If you think about it, changing from a girl into a woman is quite a huge step and requires a lot of changes. Your body is such a wonderful and powerful thing and it's actually amazing when you sit back and look at what is accomplished during puberty. Essentially your body is changing to become ready to carry a baby both physically and emotionally. In order to be prepared, your body needs to change.*

Laura asks: **"I HAVE A BUMP UNDER MY NIPPLE. IS IT SOMETHING TO WORRY ABOUT?".** *This is nothing to worry about and is your body getting ready to start growing your breasts. When your breasts start growing, they start as little buds under your nipples. They can be sore too, but that just means they are growing. It might help to buy a sports bra to help make you more comfortable. Ask your mum or Doctor if it continues to worry you just to make sure and for your own peace of mind.*

Tiffany asks: "HOW MUCH DO YOU BLEED WHEN YOU GET YOUR PERIOD?".

This will depend on what is normal for your body; usually a girl will lose between two and six tablespoons of blood each period. It's hard to tell though, and sometimes you may lose more and sometimes less. If you are concerned, talk to your parents or your doctor.

Jessica asks: "I FEEL SO SELF-CONSCIOUS ALL THE TIME AND I HATE IT?". *Puberty is a time in your life where you become aware of your body and social image. It is important to remember you are you and nobody will ever be the same as you. Try not to compare yourself to others as everyone is different. It's okay to feel self-conscious but just know that everyone feels this way at some point and doing things that make you feel happy is a great way to get your confidence up*

Casey asks: **"CAN YOU USE A TAMPON FOR DISCHARGE?"**. *It is not recommended that you use a tampon for discharge as a tampon is used to soak up a flow of liquid. Discharge is normally a small amount and a panty liner is all you should need.*

Johanna asks: **"WHAT IS PMS?"**. *PMS is an abbreviation for premenstrual syndrome. It can occur in some girls, usually the week before they get their period. You may find your breasts tender, your back aches, you have cramps, your skin breaks out and you have more than normal mood swings. All of these are a sign of PMS and are completely normal.*

Christine asks: **"WHAT IS TSS? AND WHAT HAPPENS IF A TAMPON STRING BREAKS?"**. *TSS stands for Toxic Shock Syndrome, an infection caused by bacteria in the vagina. This can occur if you leave your tampon in for too long, so remember to change it regularly and try not to sleep with a tampon in. If a tampon string breaks (which is not likely) you can easily remove the tampon by using your fingers to pull it out. If you still can't remove the tampon, just make sure you see your doctor or go to the emergency room on the same day to avoid infection.*

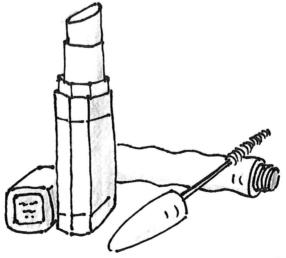

ANONYMOUS EMBARRASSING STORIES

I have put this very important section into the book in the hopes it will make you smile and laugh. These stories come from women who have come through the other side of puberty. So sit back and laugh out loud, knowing we've all been there and overcome those shocking moments when all you want to do is crawl in a hole.

For some reason, I was never told that you shouldn't wear a pad in water, so one time while my family and I were at the pool, I went in and the pad filled up with water. I looked like I was wearing a nappy and it felt like it too. Lucky my period wasn't heavy and I didn't leak everywhere. I will never make that mistake again.

I remember the day I got my period, I was with my family on holidays and I was getting dressed into my swimmers. As I looked down I noticed blood in my undies and I started screaming for my mum because I thought I was dying, she came in and reassured me and told me it was my period. I remember when she told me I wouldn't be able to swim for a few days and I burst into tears.

I got my period for the first time when I was at school, I was too embarrassed to ask anyone for a pad so I stuffed toilet paper down my undies. Luckily it was light and didn't leak, to say it was an uncomfortable day is an understatement. I never leave the house without my period kit now.

Well, I got mine at my friend's house and I thought I'd poo'd my pants. It was actually a relief to find out it was my period.

I was at my friend's house who had already gotten her period. She gave me a tampon to use and I got to the bathroom and looked at the thing and had no idea what to do with it. After several attempts at inserting one, my best friend had to come in and teach me how to do it. Yes, we are still best friends to this day and laugh about it all the time.

Let's just say I now know that you need to unwrap a tampon before you use it—eeekkkk.

Getting my period was actually exciting and my mum was so helpful and answered all my questions. We didn't however, touch on the fact you only need to wear a pad when you have your period. About a week after my period finished I asked my mum for more pads and we had a good laugh together at the fact I'd been wearing one when I didn't need to.

The first time I used a tampon I fainted, I didn't use one for a while after that"

I accidently put the tampon in the wrong hole. I lasted 5 minutes before I asked my mum for help. It hurt so bad!

When I first got my period, I thought my bottom was bleeding because I'd just done a poo, I thought I had ripped my butt open! I called my mum in who explained to me it was my period. So embarrassing but I'm glad my butt was okay.

I was with my dad when I first got my period. I was so embarrassed to ask him for something and he was just as embarrassed and said "Congratulations". My Mum then cried coz she wasn't with me for the "Special Moment".

The first time I used a tampon I used the one with the applicators but I didn't know how it worked so I ended up leaving the tampon and the cardboard applicator in for about 2hrs, it was quite painful!

FIN.

So, you've now come to the end of the book. I want to thank you and I hope you enjoyed reading it as much as I did writing it. I wrote this book hoping it would help you, inspire you and give you somewhere to turn. As girls, I think it's important that we stick together and help each other, bring each other up instead of trying to push each other down. As you grow and get older, you'll come across challenges in friendships and life. It's completely up to you how you handle these. Just remember to be kind, to love each other and know that you can empower and inspire each other to reach your goals and fulfil your dreams! The world is at your feet, enjoy it. I would love you all to be part of my journey, I'm constantly posting and blogging about my life and everyday challenges and opinions. I appreciate all your support and love and that so many of you have entrusted me with your questions. On the next page are all my social media handles, let's work together to change the world and be there for each other.

OTHER BOOKS
BY ROSIE LUIK

'An IVF Story'

'21st Century Guide to the Birds and the Bees'

'Ipswich Lets Play'

Books are available to buy at:

www.rosieluik.com

Love, Rosie
Australia

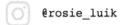 @rosie_luik

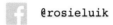 @rosieluik

 @rosieluik

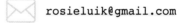 rosieluik@gmail.com

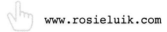 www.rosieluik.com

Made in the USA
Las Vegas, NV
31 August 2021